# Reading for Comprehension
## READINESS

Book 1

Written by Arlene Capriola and Rigmor Swensen
Illustrated by Laurie Conley

ISBN 978-0-8454-3855-8

Copyright © 2007 The Continental Press, Inc.

No part of this publication may be reproduced in any form or by any means, electronic, mechanical, photocopying, recording, or otherwise, without the prior written permission of the publisher. All rights reserved. Printed in the United States of America.

Continental Press

# What do ants do?

Ants are very little.
They have 6 legs.
Ants can be red or black.

Ants make ant hills.
They live in the ant hills.
They dig paths.
They make rooms.
Ants are very busy.

  Reading for Comprehension Readiness © The Continental Press, Inc. Do not duplicate.

**Circle the letter for the right answer.**

1. This story is about _____.

     **a** dogs        **b** ants        **c** cats

2. Ants can be _____.

     **a** blue        **b** green        **c** red

3. Ants live in ant _____.

     **a** hills        **b** caves        **c** towns

4. You can tell that ants _____.

     **a** are sad        **b** work hard        **c** play a lot

**Write a word from the story to finish the sentence.**

The ant hill has many _____.

# How do worms help us?

Worms are thin and soft.
They have no legs.
They dig in the dirt.
They dig up and down.

Worms help to mix up the dirt.
That helps plants grow.
We eat the plants.
So worms help us.

  Reading for Comprehension Readiness © The Continental Press, Inc. Do not duplicate.

**Circle the letter for the right answer.**

1. The story is about _____.

   a  birds          b  worms          c  snakes

2. Worms _____ us.

   a  help           b  bite           c  like

3. Worms can _____.

   a  fly            b  jump           c  dig

4. You can tell from the story that worms _____.

   a  can not walk                     b  dig up plants

             c  do not sleep

**Write a word from the story to finish the sentence.**

Worms dig in the _____.

# What makes a skunk safe?

This animal looks like a small cat.
It is black and white.
It has a long tail.
It is a skunk.

A skunk can make a bad smell.
The smell lasts a long time.
Other animals stay away.
We stay away, too.
The skunk is safe.

 © The Continental Press, Inc. Do not duplicate.

**Circle the letter for the right answer.**

1. This is a story about a small _____.

   **a** fish          **b** animal          **c** bug

2. Other animals _____ the skunk.

   **a** stay away from          **b** play with

   **c** look for

3. We do not like this animal's _____.

   **a** colors          **b** food          **c** smell

4. You can tell that skunks do not _____.

   **a** like the smell          **b** have babies

   **c** need to run away

**Write a word from the story to finish the sentence.**

A skunk looks like a _____.

# How does the cow help her baby?

A mother cow has a baby.
She licks it to make it clean.
Then she helps it to stand up.
She gives it her milk.

A baby cow is called a calf.
Soon the calf can eat.
It will eat a lot.
Then it will be as big as its mother.

© The Continental Press, Inc. Do not duplicate.

**Circle the letter for the right answer.**

1. This story tells about the _____.

   a pig        b cow        c bug

2. The mother cow _____ her new baby.

   a hugs      b leaves      c cleans

3. She gives the little calf _____.

   a grass      b milk      c eggs

4. You can tell that a calf will be a _____.

   a cow      b horse      c skunk

**Write a word from the story to finish the sentence.**

The calf needs help to _____ up.

# What can a firefly do?

It is summer.
The sun goes down.
It is dark.
A bug flies by you.

The bug lights up.
The light goes on and off.
What is the bug?
The bug is a firefly.

Can you trap it?

  Reading for Comprehension Readiness © The Continental Press, Inc. Do not duplicate.

**Circle the letter for the right answer.**

1. This story is about a _____.

   **a** bug      **b** bird      **c** worm

2. This bug can _____.

   **a** jump      **b** sing      **c** fly

3. In this story, the light comes from the _____.

   **a** sky      **b** bug      **c** sun

4. You can tell that boys and girls may _____ the firefly.

   **a** hear      **b** catch      **c** help

**Write a word from the story to finish the sentence.**

You can see a firefly when it is _____.

© The Continental Press, Inc. Do not duplicate.

Go To Fun Page 28   

# Are all horses big?

Most horses are big.
But one horse is very little.
It can be as small as a dog.

The little horse is a good pet.
It likes to run and play.
It can live on a farm.

The little horse is too small to ride.
But it can pull a cart.
The little horse is lots of fun.

  Reading for Comprehension Readiness

© The Continental Press, Inc. Do not duplicate.

**Circle the letter for the right answer.**

1. This story is about a _____ horse.

   a big         b little        c toy

2. The little horse can be as small as a
   _____.

   a cat         b dog        c bug

3. You can tell that <u>little</u> means the same
   as _____.

   a funny       b good       c small

4. The little horse can not pull a _____
   around.

   a house      b cart       c sled

**Write a word from the story to finish the sentence.**

The little horse likes to _____.

# What is a school of fish?

Big fish like to swim alone.
But little fish swim together.
We call them a school of fish.
A school can have many fish.

The fish in a school help each other.
They look for food together.
They look out for big fish.
A school is like one giant fish!

Reading for Comprehension Readiness © The Continental Press, Inc. Do not duplicate.

**Circle the letter for the right answer.**

1. This story is about _____.

   **a** fish       **b** giants       **c** toys

2. In the sea, small fish swim _____.

   **a** alone       **b** on top       **c** together

3. A school can have _____ fish.

   **a** no       **b** one       **c** many

4. You can tell that small fish _____ the school.

   **a** hate       **b** need       **c** eat

**Write a word from the story to finish the sentence.**

Many fish swim together in a _____.

# Where is your shadow?

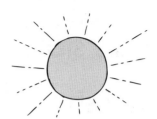

You can make a shadow.
Go outside in the sun.
Turn your back to the sun.
You can see your shadow.

Your shadow jumps when you jump.
It sits when you sit.
It goes where you go.

Try this.
Go in your house.
Look for your shadow.
Your shadow is gone!

  Reading for Comprehension Readiness     © The Continental Press, Inc. Do not duplicate.

**Circle the letter for the right answer.**

1. This story is about _____.

   a the sun                 b your shadow

            c the morning

2. When it is _____, you can see your shadow.

   a dark        b raining        c sunny

3. Your shadow _____ when you skip.

   a sits        b skips        c runs

4. You can not see your shadow in the house because there is no _____.

   a sun        b bird        c tree

**Write a word from the story to finish the sentence.**

_____

Your _____ does what you do.

# What is our flag?

Our flag is red and white and blue.
It has stars and stripes.
There are 50 stars.
There are 13 stripes.

The flag stands for our country.
We fly the flag on a pole.
We put the flag up in the morning.
We take it down after dark.
Look for the flag by your school.

Reading for Comprehension Readiness

© The Continental Press, Inc. Do not duplicate.

**Circle the letter for the right answer.**

1. This story tells about our _____.

   **a** cat       **b** flag       **c** house

2. The flag stands for our _____.

   **a** school       **b** pets       **c** country

3. Our flag has _____ colors.

   **a** three       **b** six       **c** ten

4. You can tell that our country _____.

   **a** has many flags       **b** has one flag

          **c** needs a new flag

**Write a word from the story to finish the sentence.**

Our flag has stripes and _____.

# How much is a penny?

A penny is one cent.
You need 5 pennies for a nickel.
You need 10 pennies for a dime.
You need 100 pennies for a dollar.

It is fun to save pennies.
You can put them in a bank.
You can count them.
Soon you can buy a toy.

Reading for Comprehension Readiness
© The Continental Press, Inc. Do not duplicate.

**Circle the letter for the right answer.**

1. This story tells about a _____.

   a truck      b toy      c penny

2. A penny is one _____.

   a cent      b bag      c day

3. A _____ is the same as 5 pennies.

   a cent      b nickel      c dime

4. To get a dollar, you need _____ 10 pennies.

   a just      b less than      c more than

**Write a word from the story to finish the sentence.**

_____

You can save pennies in a _____.

© The Continental Press, Inc. Do not duplicate.

# Can a doctor be a farmer too?

Doctor Mike takes care of sick kids.
After work, he goes home.
Where does he live?

Doctor Mike lives on a farm.
He grows corn and beans there.
He has lots of chickens, too.
He must feed them and get the eggs.
It is hard work.

Doctor Mike likes to be a doctor.
He likes to be a farmer, too.
So he does both jobs!

  Reading for Comprehension Readiness © The Continental Press, Inc. Do not duplicate.

**Circle the letter for the right answer.**

1. This story is about a man with _____.

   a  a dog          b  two jobs          c  a big house

2. Doctor Mike's home is a _____.

   a  ranch          b  zoo              c  farm

3. Doctor Mike <u>takes</u> <u>care</u> <u>of</u> sick kids.
   That means he _____ them.

   a  helps          b  needs            c  likes

4. You can tell that Doctor Mike grows lots
   of _____.

   a  flowers        b  food             c  fruit

**Write a word from the story to finish the sentence.**

Doctor Mike lives on a _____.

# Does the Earth stop?

We live on the Earth.
It is our home.
The Earth is like a big round ball.

We do not feel the Earth move.
But it does.
It spins like a top.
Around and around it goes.
It does not stop.

In the day time, we face the sun.
The sun gives us light.
Then we turn away from the sun.
It gets dark. It is night. We go to sleep.

Reading for Comprehension Readiness © The Continental Press, Inc. Do not duplicate.

**Circle the letter for the right answer.**

1. The story is about how the Earth _____.

   a stands still                  b is up

               c goes around

2. The Earth moves like a _____.

   a ball         b top         c hat

3. The _____ gives us light.

   a sun         b Earth         c ball

4. It is dark when we _____ the sun.

   a can feel                 b can not see

             c can find

**Write a word from the story to finish the sentence.**

_____

The Earth does not _____.

# Fun Page

## WHAT DO ANTS DO?

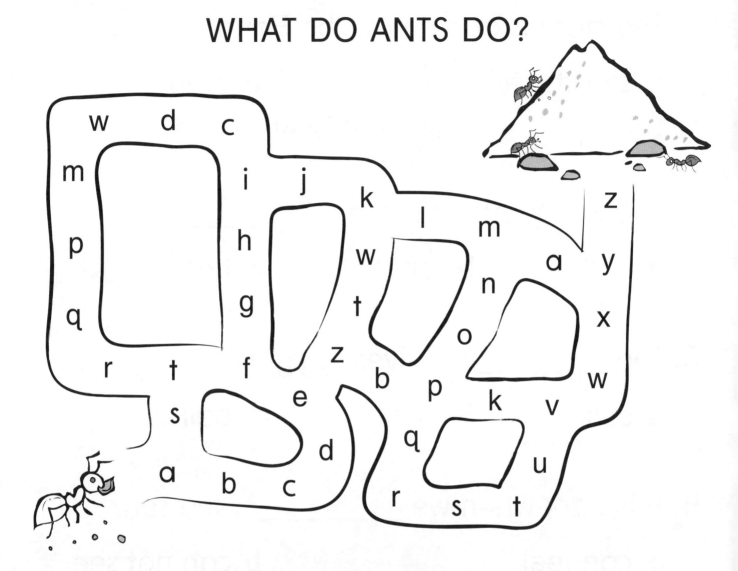

- ⊙ The ant wants to go home. Help it find the way.

- ⊙ Go the a-b-c way.

- ⊙ Color the ant red.

- ⊙ Color the ant hill black.

  Skills: Sequencing and Following Directions © The Continental Press, Inc. Do not duplicate.

## WHAT MAKES A SKUNK SAFE?

**skunk**                    **cat**

⊙  A skunk looks like a cat. Which one am I?

| I am black and white. | I am a |
| I can make a bad smell. | _____ |
| You run away from me. | _____ . |

| I can be lots of colors. | I am a |
| You like to pet me. | _____ |
| I can live in a house. | _____ . |

⊙  Color the pictures.

© The Continental Press, Inc. Do not duplicate.        Skills: Visual Discrimination and Following Directions

# WHEN CAN A FIREFLY DO?

⊙ Put a ○ around the picture that tells:

## The firefly is under the boy.

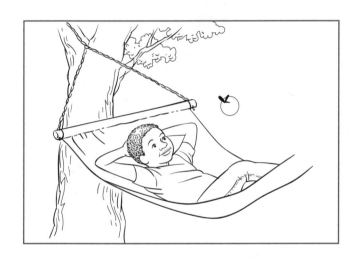

## The bug's light is off.

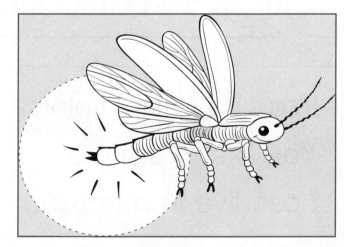

⊙ Color the pictures.

  Skills: Observing and Following Directions

© The Continental Press, Inc. Do not duplicate.

# Fun Page

## WHAT IS A SCHOOL OF FISH?

⊙ Put 1, 2, or 3 in the box to show the story.

**First,** the fish swim in a school.

**Then,** they see a big, big fish.

**Last,** they hide in back of the plants.

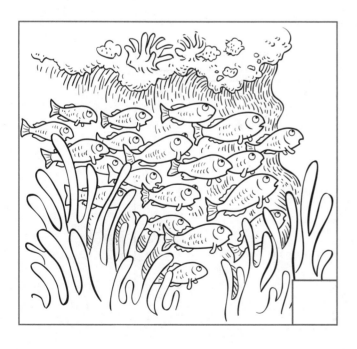

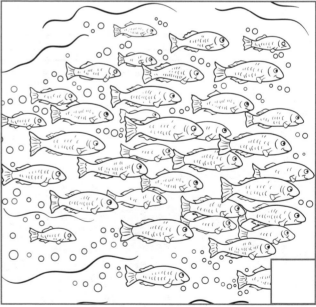

⊙ Color the pictures.

© The Continental Press, Inc. Do not duplicate.

# WHAT IS OUR FLAG?

Can you make this flag?

⊙ Make the stripes red and white.

⊙ Put lots of stars (✳) in the big box.

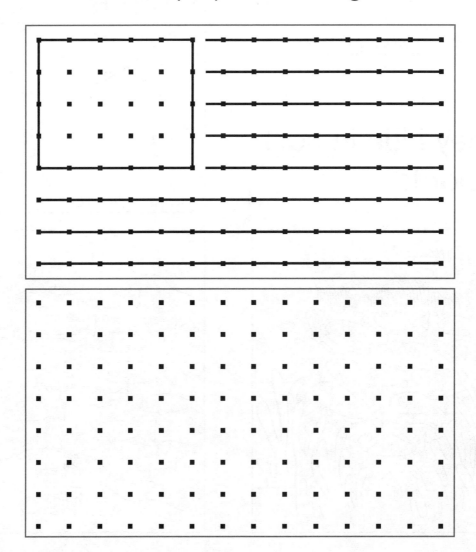

⊙ Color the big box blue.

Skills: Geo Pattern and Following Directions   © The Continental Press, Inc. Do not duplicate.

## HOW MUCH IS A PENNY?

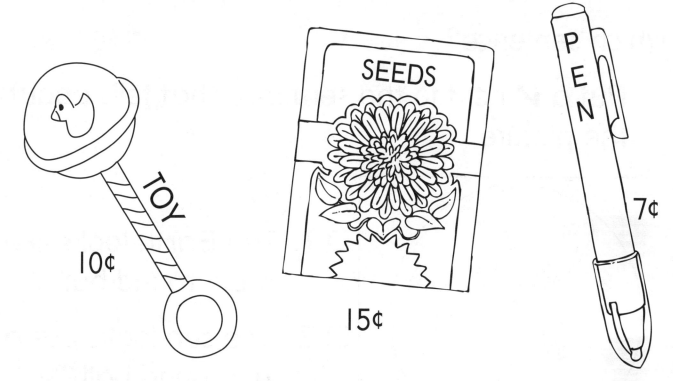

⊙ We go to the store.

Mom likes flowers. Seeds are _____ ¢.

We get a toy for the baby. I give the man

one _____.

We buy a pen for Dad. I give the man one

_____ and two _____.

⊙ Color the pictures.

## DOES THE EARTH STOP?

Which sentence?

⊙ Put a ✔ next to the sentence that tells about the picture.

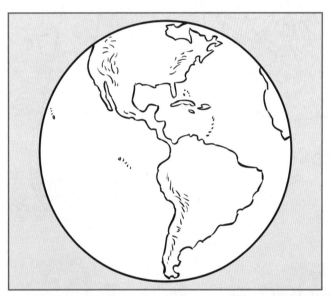

❑ 1. The Earth looks like a big round ball.

❑ 2. The sun looks like a big round ball.

❑ 1. We face the sun in the day.

❑ 2. We turn away from the sun at night.

Skills: Sequencing and Following Directions    © The Continental Press, Inc. Do not duplicate.